Crypt

of the

Vampire

DELUXE ADVENTURE MODULE
The Lord Vandric Chronicles V.3

An Adventure Module for 1 Player
For the Hammer + Cross RPG
Designed by Noah Patterson

Hammer

Cross

Crypt of the Vampire
The Lord VanDrac Chronicles V.3
Copyright © 2020 Noah Patterson
ISBN: 9798694597883

Find us on DriveThru RPG
Or at MicroRPG.weebly.com

Cover Artwork by Dean Spencer Art

Map Art by Patrick E. Pullen

STOP!

DON'T BUY THIS BOOK!
At least, not yet.

The basic rules for the Micro Chapbook RPG
system and Hammer + Cross found in this book
can be downloaded for FREE through
DriveThruRPG.com in the Manor of Blood book.
Give the system a try before you buy.

With that in mind, this Deluxe Adventure
Module includes everything you need to play
the game.

You don't need any other book to experience
the game!

Contents

Section 1.0

What is Crypt of the Vampire?

Crypt of the Vampire is an adventure module for the Hammer + Cross Roleplaying game system and is the third volume in the Lord VanDrac Chronicles story arc. Each volume in the 5 book series stands on its own, but all connect to create a greater campaign. Therefore, this adventure can be played on its own or as part of the larger VanDrac story arc.

This book includes the basic rules to allow you to play the game. However, the Hammer + Cross core rulebook will go into greater detail on all elements of the game. Hammer + Cross uses the Micro Chapbook RPG system and, therefore, this book can be combined with any other books or genres in the same system.

For those new to the system, Micro Chapbook RPG is an ultra-rules light fantasy-based game designed specifically for the solitaire gamer in mind--but is adaptable for co-op play as well as traditional Game Master driven gameplay.

Hammer + Cross is a Gothic Horror rendition of the traditionally fantasy-based game system. In Hammer + Cross, you take on the role of vampire and monster hunters in an alternate version of late 1800s Victorian Europe where evil abounds. The game is strongly influenced by the Hammer Horror films of the 60s and 70s.

Section 2.0
What Do You Need?

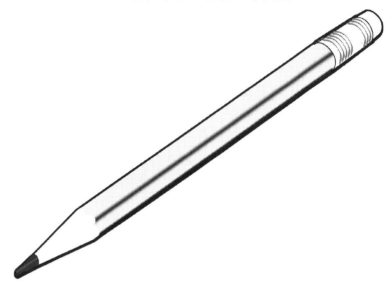

To play this adventure you will need:

- A Pencil and Eraser
- A Sheet of Graph Paper
- A Character Sheet
- 2 Six-Sided Dice
- This Adventure Book
- The Hammer + Cross Core Rulebook (Optional).

Section 3.0

Rules Basics

Hammer + Cross is an ultra-simple roleplaying game that can be played solo (or with a traditional GM if you so wish). In the next few pages, you will find the basic rules for the game system:

What You Need: 2 six-sided dice, graph paper, notepaper/character sheet, a pencil w/eraser, Scenario Maps/Sticker, this chapbook.

Rolling: During play, you always roll 1D6, trying to score equal to or lower than your stat score. If you are proficient, roll 2 dice and take the better result of the 2. 1 always succeeds. 6 always fails. (NOTE: When you see 1D3 it means you roll a die and half the result rounding up. 1D2 means: Odds = 1, Evens = 2.)

Characters: To create a character, do the following:

1. **STATS:** You have 4 statistics. **ST**rength, **DE**xterity, **WI**ts, **CH**arisma. You have 7 points to assign between them as you see fit (9 for an easier game). No stat can have a score lower than 1 or higher than 4 at this point.

2. **CLASS:** Choose a class. There are 4 to choose from. Each one will make you proficient in one area.
   a. **Soldier:** Proficient in ST
   b. **Hunter:** Proficient in DE
   c. **Nurse/Doctor:** Proficient in WI
   d. **Priest/Nun:** Proficient in CH

3. **ORDER:** Choose an Order to join. Your Order grants you a +1 bonus to one stat.
   a. **Order of the Hammer:** +1 ST
   b. **Order of the Dagger:** +1 DE
   c. **Order of the Cross:** +1 WI
   d. **Order of the Sun:** +1 CH
4. **HEALTH, WILL, & FAITH:** Your health is your ST+DE+20. Your will is your WI+CH+20. Your Faith is your Wits + 20 (+ 25 if you're a Priest/Nun).

Weapons: Roll 2D6 to determine your money. You may buy equipment now. Weapons have a damage rating and a cost in pounds (£). Below are some basic starter weapons, both ranged and melee. You may have 2 melee and 1 ranged at any given time. You may buy these and others in town as well.

Melee Weapons			Ranged Weapons		
Dagger	1	1g	Holy Cross	1	2g
Wooden Stake	1D3	2g	Holy Water Sprayer	1D3	3g
Hammer	1D3+1	3g	Rusty Revolver	1D3+1	5g
Cane Sword	1D6	4g	Blessed Long Whip	1D6	6g
Silver Sword	1D6+1	5g	Crossbow	1D6+1	7g

Armor and Items: Armor grants the wearer a boost to their health, will, or both. Other items such and food and potions can be used to restore lost health and will. On the next page are some basic starter items and armors. You may buy these and others in town as well.

Armor			Items		
Shield	+3H	1£	(2) Bread Crust	1D3 H	1£
Top Hat	+3W	1£	(3) Wine	1D3 W	1£
Black Cloak	+6H	2£	(4) Steak Meal	1D6 H	2£
Chainmail	+6W	2£	(5) Holy Water	1D6 W	2£
Blessed Robes	+6HW	3£	(6) Miracle	FULL HW	6£

Generating Rooms: Begin by choosing a random square on the graph paper and generating the first room. To generate a room, roll 2D6. The number rolled in the number of squares in the room. These can be drawn in any way, shape, or form so long as they are orthogonally connected. Next, roll 1D3 (1D6 divided by 2 rounded up). This is the number of NEW doors in the room (not including the door you just came through). Draw small rectangles to represent the doors along any single square's edge to designate an exit.

Room Type: Each newly generated room has a type. Roll 1D6 on the scenario Room Chart to determine the type. Note this in the room with the type's letter code as listed on the chart.

Doorways: Next, you will choose one door to move through into the next room. Roll 1D6 to determine the door type. After moving, generate the new room. (This chart is also provided in each scenario).

(5-6)	Unlocked	Move through freely.
(4)	Stuck	Must make a ST check to get through. Lose 1 WILL to reroll and try again.
(3)	Locked	Must make a WI check to get through. Lose 1 WILL to reroll and try again.
(1-2)	Trapped	Must make a WI check to disarm and move. If you fail, take 1D3 damage but still move through.

Monsters: After Entering any room. Roll to generate the monsters in the room. Roll once for the monster type (on the scenario Monster Chart) and a second time for the number of that monster. Each monster has a Max number of that type that can appear in a room, a Health Damage, a Will Damage, and a Life Force. **Vampires** also have two additional special stats:

- **Bloodletting (BL):** Each time the player rolls a 6 during a melee attack (an instant failure), the vampire bites them and drinks their blood. The BL is how much LF it regains.
- **Power (P):** This is the mental strength of the vampire. It is the amount of faith the player will lose if they fail during the Faith check.

Fighting: To fight the monsters in your room, follow these steps in order:
1. **Bravery:** Make a CH check. If you pass, gain 1 Will. If you fail, you lose Will according to the monster's W DMG. If your Will is ever 0, all rolls take a +1 modifier. (A roll of 1 STILL always succeeds)
2. **Ranged Attack:** IF the room is 4 squares or larger you may make a ranged attack. Roll a DE check. If you succeed, apply weapon damage to the monster's LF.

3. **Melee Attack:** You MUST now make a melee attack using a ST check. If you succeed, apply the weapon's damage to the monster's LF. If you fail, roll the H DMG for one monster and apply it to your health. If you have a second melee weapon equipped, attack again.

4. **Repeat:** Repeat this entire process until either you die or you've killed all the monsters in the room. Run away with a successful CH roll.

Faith Check: After battle, if the player was bitten by a vampire during combat, that player makes a WI check. If the player fails, they lose Faith in the amount of the vampire's power. The player may spend 1 Willpower to reroll this check. If Faith reaches 0, the character dies and becomes a vampire.

Search: After battle roll 1D6. If you get 1 through 5 you earn that much money. If you roll a six, roll on the Items table included in the scenario (or the one here in this section. The number to the left of each item is the search roll number). If you roll a 1 on the items chart you find nothing.

The Boss: The boss of the dungeon will not appear until you've encountered all the other monsters in the scenario at least once. Additionally, it will only appear in specific room types as outlined in each scenario. If you roll the boss when it can't appear, reroll. Once the boss is defeated, the game ends.

Alternate Boss Rule: (for potentially quicker games) Keep track of each monster you kill during the dungeon. After each battle is won, roll 2D6. If the roll is LOWER than the number of monsters killed during the dungeon, the boss can now have a chance of appearing. The boss will only appear in specific areas, as designated by the scenario rules. If you roll the boss when it can't appear, reroll.

Leveling Up: In between games you may spend 100 gold to add +1 to one stat (or 50 for an easier game). No stat can be higher than 5. For an easier game, simply level up whenever you defeat a boss. You may also buy new equipment. You may only have 2 melee and 1 ranged weapon at a time.

Section 4.0

Adventure Background

The headquarters of the Order which you are a part of is eerily quiet as you arrive back from your most recent vampire hunting excursion. While the old renovated townhome, tucked away on a lesser traveled street of London, is never a truly vibrant place, it seems almost dead. The sound of the rain outside pitters down outside, echoing strangely through the building.

Heading up the staircase, you approach your superior's office at the head of the landing. Knocking lighty, you hear him grunt--his way of saying to come in.

"Finally," he says from behind his huge wooden desk as you step inside, "it took you long enough to get here."

You inform him that you just got back from the countryside where you fought off some ancient undead vampire knights and found more clues about this Lord VanDrac.

"I'm well aware," he notes impatiently. "I've been doing some investigation into this man myself," he informs you.

This is a surprise, considering he had seemed disinterested when you first shared your concern about Lord VanDrac. You'd asked to be given permission to dig deeper into VanDrac's past, but your superior had refused and sent you on another errand. It had just so happened that this new errand also seemed to connect to VanDrac--but now you begin to wonder if your superior knew this all along.

"I believe I've located the final resting place, or at least last recorded resting place, of one Lord VanDrac. It's a cemetery here in London." He pauses. "I want you to check it out. See if the old Lord, or at least some part of him, is indeed still in his grave . . . If not, we may have a dire problem on our hands."

Section 5.0

The Groundskeeper

You are growing tired of the constant rain, especially when you know you will be stuck outside for hours investigating a cemetery. The carriage ride over to the location is short, too short, and you are dreading stepping out into the downpour.

"Out," the rude carriage driver shouts. You begin to wish the Order would find a more reliable carriage service as you climb down into the chilling rain. At the very least the driver didn't drop you off in the middle of the woods like last time.

Standing in front of two huge, tall wrought-iron gates, you stare in at a mess of graves and foliage beyond. Stepping forward, you push on the gate only to realize it has a padlock and chain attached to it.

"Can I help you, governor?" an elderly man with stark white hair asks, bundled up in his coat and ragged brown top hat.

You may now ask the old man the following questions:

- **Who are you?** "Well, I'm the groundskeeper here at the cemetery. I was just checking the gate to make sure no one had gone in. Sorry to say, the cemetery is closed for the time being."
- **Why is the cemetary closed?** There have been some strange things going on of late. I keep catching people sneaking in after dark when the gates are locked for

the night. We've been having occasional trouble with grave robbers, so I reported it to the coppers. When they had a look, they found a dead body inside," he chuckles, "well, I mean a fresh dead body that shouldn't have been there. Seems the young lady was murdered, completely drained of blood." He shivers. "Spooky stuff if you ask me."

- **If you ask about the grave robbers.** "Someone has been robbing graves. The funny thing is they never take anything of value. They've only ever taken body parts. They must be demented."

- **Can you let me inside?** "I don't see how I can do that. The police asked me to keep it closed for now." You may now make a CH check to get him to open the gate. If you pass, read the text box below. If you fail, you must spend 1 Willpower to try again. You may also spend 1 pound beforehand to subtract −1 from the roll.

"Well, I suppose it won't hurt to let you in. You seem a nice enough person." With that he unlocks the padlock, lets you in, and then shuts the gate, locking it behind you. "Have a pleasant time," he chuckles evilly, leaving you alone.

Section 6.0

The Cemetery

Grave stones, mausoleums, and an overgrowth of trees, bushes, and ivy make this cemetery extremely claustrophobic. Hundreds of graves mark the land, all shoved into close proximity.

You may be locked in here, but at least you have a chance to search for Lord VanDrac's final resting place. According to the instructions given to you by the superior, he lays beneath the earth in a crypt. Now, the only trouble for you, is finding the entrance to the crypt.

However, you are keeping your guard up. You know there may be vampires or vampire minions lurking here.

Cemetery Special Rules:

Locating the Crypt: While in the cemetery, you are trying to locate the entrance to Lord VanDrac's crypt. Upon entering each new area, but before rolling an area type, make a WITS check. If you pass, mark that you've earned 1 Investigation Point. Then roll 2D6. If the result is lower than the number of Investigation Points, you've located the Crypt Entrance. This room is a Mausoleum type and the boss appears hee.

Doorways and Rooms: The term doorways is replaced with "Exits" for the cemetery. Rooms are replaced with "Areas." When mapping outdoor dungeons, there is an added element to creating areas. Each time you generate a new area, and after rolling the exits, the area directly around it must be shaded in to show the graves and foliage--all adjacent squares except the ones leading to exits are shaded.

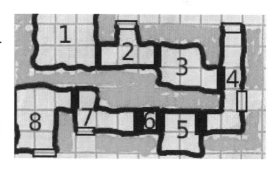

Cemetery Exits

6	Clear	Move through freely.
4-5	Muck	Must make a ST check to tread through the mud. If you fail, lose 1 WILL and reroll and try again.
2-3	Blocked	A bramble of twisted ivy or a broken tombstone blocks the way. Make a DE check to leap over. If you fail, lose 1 HEALTH and reroll to try again.
1	Hidden Open Grave	An open grave has been covered over with ivy and leaves to mask the hole. Make a WITS check to see the hole before falling in or take 1D3 falling damage. Then, if you fall in, you must make a DE check to climb out. If you fail, lose 1 willpower and try again. If you are out of willpower, lose 1 health and try again instead.

Cemetery Area Types

1	Clear	C	This area has grass and clear paths. No effect.
2	Mossy	Mo	The graves and ground here are covered in soft, wet, moss. This makes the ground slick. Add +1 on all DE checks.
3	Uneven Ground	U	The ground here is uneven, making you believe graves have been dug up and covered over again. As a result, you sink into the earth with each step. Add +1 on all ST checks.
4	Foggy	F	This area is shrouded in fog. It makes it difficult to see. +1 on all Ranged Attacks.
5	Mausoleum	Ma	Attach a 2x2 room to this area. Add in the door connecting the area and the Mausoleum anywhere you wish. The Mauzoleum and original area count as 1 area together. In addition to the normal monster roll, there are also 1D3 Rotting Zombies here.
6	Overgrown	O	This area is overgrown with brambles and ivy. This makes melee attacks more difficult. +1 on all melee attacks and −1 damage to a minimum of 1.

Cemetery Monsters

#	Monster	Max	H-DMG	W-DMG	LF
1	Bat	4	1D2	1D3+1	3
2	Rotting Corpse	3	1D3	1	4
3	Demented Grave Digger	1	1D6	1D6	5
4	Crawling Hand	6	1D3	1D6	3
5	Vampiric Skeleton	3	1D6	1D6	10
6	Vampire Guard*	1	1D6	1D3+1	20

Vampiric Powers

	Bloodletting	Power
Vampiric Skeleton	1D2	1
Vampire Guard	1D3	1D2

*The boss of this Dungeon is the Vampire Guard. He is accompanied by 3 Rotting corpses. Once he is defeated, you may move into the crypt entrance.

Section 7.0

The Forgotten Crypt

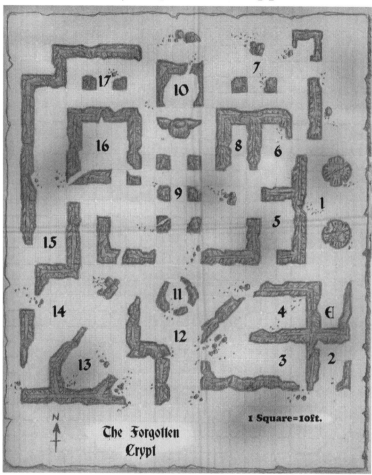

The Forgotten Crypt

1 Square=10ft.

The stench of wet decay invades your nose as you descend the stairs and open the doorway into the old forgotten crypt. It is clear that no one "living" has been down here in some time. The floors are wet earth. Water from the rain drips down from the ceiling. The once proud walls are crumbling. There are holes in walls in places and some walls have come down altogether.

However, this is supposedly where Lord VanDrac was buried. The problem is, the place is in such a shambles, you fear finding the original grave may be difficult. You even wonder if the Lord VanDrac has more followers or minions who came down here and already ransacked the place.

The Forgotten Crypt Special Rules:

The Forgotten Crypt is a preconstructed dungeon map. Each room has a number. These numbers correspond with a sheet of numbered "room tokens" included at the back of this book. You will need to copy the page and cut the tokens out. You can also make your own. They simply need to be uniform on the back and numbered 1–17 on the front.

Once the tokens are cut out, shuffle them all and draw one randomly without looking and place it aside. This is where Lord VanDrac's coffin is.

You start at the entryway labeled **E.** Whenever you move from one numbered area on the map to another, make a door roll as usual. Doors here are actually passageways. When entering a new area, you will skip the steps for generating rooms and # of doors and instead move directly to the room type step. Proceed with gameplay as normal. Once all monsters in a room are defeated, you will then do the following:

1. Make a WITS check to investigate the area for clues.
2. If you are successful, draw one random room token. Whatever number is listed you now know doesn't contain the coffin.
3. You may then choose if you will declare where Lord VanDrac's coffin. If you do, declare which number contains Lord VanDrac. Then reveal the room token you previously set aside.
   a. If you are correct, you will gain an upper hand for the final battle. Make your way to the room in question. Once there, you will gain −1 toward every attack roll and +1 to every damage roll.
   b. If you are incorrect, you will receive a penalty for the final

battle. Make your way to the room in question. Once there, you will lose +1 on every attack roll and −1 (to a minimum of 1) for damage rolls.

c. In either case, once you've attempted your decision at the coffin location, the number of room tokens you've looked at prior to choosing is added to the boss's Life Force. (Example: If you looked at 13 tokens, you'd add 13 to the Life Force).

FINALLY: When you make it to the room with the coffin, you will jump to section 7.1 and read the special text for the final room of this dungeon.

Crypt Passageways		
6	Open	Move through freely.
4-5	Blocked	Must make a ST check to get through. Lose 1 WILL to reroll and try again.
1-3	Collapsing Ceiling	Must make a DE check to dodge falling debris or take 1D6 H-DMG.

Crypt Area Types		
1	Empty **E**	This area has nothing of significance at first glance. No effect.
2	Muddy **M**	The ground in this area is very wet and muddy. It makes it hard to move and adds +1 to all DE checks.
3	Flooded **F**	This room has flooded with rainwater. The stagnant water is filthy and difficult to move through. Each time you fail a DE check in this room, you will take 1 H-DMG.
4	Collapsed **C**	The room has already collapsed and there is rubble everywhere. It makes melee attacks difficult, adding +1 to the roll. You also must subtract −1 from the damage rolls.
5	Rotting Coffins **R**	This room is filled with rotting coffins. They are aged and smell and make the search for the coffin you are seeking difficult. +1 to all WITS checks in this room.
6	Scattered Bones **S**	The bones of the dead have been scattered everywhere in this room. Either grave robbers or rats are responsible, maybe both. In addition to the regular monster roll, you also run into 1D3 sewer rats.

Crypt Monsters					
#	Monster	Max	H-DMG	W-DMG	LF
1	Sewer Rat	5	1D2	1D3	4
2	Vampire Bat	4	1D3	1D3+1	3
3	Bloated Corpse +	3	1D3	1D3	4
4	Vampiric Skeleton	3	1D6	1D6	10
5	Child Vampire #	2	1D6	1D6+1	15
6	Vampire Knight	1	1D6+1	1D6	20

+The Bloated Corpse, when killed, explodes. Make a DE check to dodge it or take 1D6 H-DMG.

#The Vampire Child is horrifying and all Bravery rolls against it are made at +1.

Vampiric Powers		
	Bloodletting	Power
Vampiric Skeleton	1D2	1
Child Vampire	1	1
Vampire Knight	1D3	1D2

The boss of this dungeon isn't listed here. Instead, the boss will be listed in section 7.1.

Section 7.0

Lord VanDrac's Coffin

Rummaging through countless coffins, you finally come upon one with a familiar crest. The Raven you remember of Lord VanDrac's crest is on the lid of this coffin. You've finally found his resting place.

Digging your fingers under the coffin lid, you pry it open and jump back, wooden stake at the ready.

However, to your horror, the casket is empty.

A cackling that is all too familiar comes from behind you. Turning, you see a short hunchbacked man you'd hoped was dead. "Father Tavers," you spit out.

"You fool. The Lord is long gone. His bones are on their way to America right now, where his followers will resurrect him once and for all."

He steps toward you, drawing out a long sword with a red hilt. "Too bad you won't be there to witness his miraculous return." He lunges at you.

You must now defeat Father Tavers. You may also choose to attack the coffin. The coffin has 15 LF. If you miss an attack against it, either ranged or melee, Father Tavers deals damage to you. If you break down the coffin, Father Tavers's damage scores will be halved.

Once you have depleted his Life Force, head to Section 8.0: Finishing the Adventure.

Monster	Max	H-DMG	W-DMG	LF
Father Tavers	1	2D6	2D6	20

Father Tavers Vampiric Power	Bloodletting	Power
	1D3	1D3

Section 8.0

Ending the Adventure

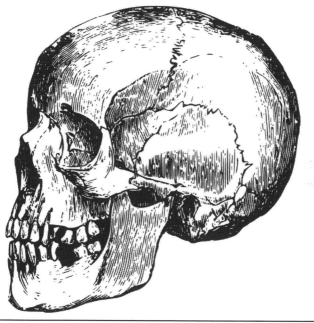

Striking one final blow against Father Tavers, the hunchback lets out a bellowing scream and attempts to grab onto you. His hand clutches at your breast coat but you push him off. He collapses into a nearby rotting coffin . . . with something he stole from you in his hand. It is the rib bone of Lord VanDrac you got on your last assignment. The lid slams shut with a thud. Before your very eyes, you watch the coffin sink into the mud and vanish beneath the earth.

You hope that is the last you'll see of him, but somehow you feel like this isn't over yet.

From what Father Tavers said, you gather that he and other followers of VanDrac have been tracking down all of the Lord's bones with plans to resurrect him. Any smart vampire hunter would likely scatter the bones of a formidable vampire all over the world to prevent such a horrific occurrence.

However, if this cult of followers were determined enough, they would figure out how to get all the bones. The only one you'd managed to find and hold onto was now buried in the mud.

If the rest of the Lord's bones were on a ship for America, that could mean the cult was planning on unleashing hell on the new world. Your only hope is to catch that ship before it leaves docks. Gathering your courage, you rush out of the dirty crypt and back into the open air of the cemetery.

A carriage pulls up at the gates, which sit miraculously open. "To the docks," you tell the driver.

Room Number Tokens

Hammer✠Cross

Character Record Sheet

Name: **Order:**   **Class:**

STATS

St   De   Wi   Ch

Proficiency:

WEAPONS

Ranged: **Melee:**

ARMOR   ITEMS

WILL   HEALTH   FAITH   £

Made in the USA
Monee, IL
12 August 2021